Anthem II
Let thy hand be strengthened
No. 1

FOUR CORONATION ANTHEMS

G. F. HANDEL

Anthem I

Zadok the priest

Printed in Great Britain
OXFORD UNIVERSITY PRESS, MUSIC DEPARTMENT, GREAT CLARENDON STREET, OXFORD OX2 6DP

No. 2

No. 3

Anthem III
The King shall rejoice
No. 1

No. 2

*Allegro

* Throughout this movement, both ♪♪ and ♪.♪ may be performed ♪³♪.

No. 3

No. 4

Anthem IV

My heart is inditing

No. 1

No. 2

No. 3

No. 4

ISBN 978-0-19-335270-4